THE

WINDOWSILL GARDENER

First published in Great Britain in 2021 by
Michael O'Mara Books Limited
9 Lion Yard
Tremadoc Road
London SW4 7NQ

A CIP catalogue record for this book is available from
the British Library.

Papers used by Michael O'Mara Books Limited are
natural, recyclable products made from wood grown
in sustainable forests. The manufacturing processes
conform to the environmental regulations of the
country of origin.

ISBN: 978-1-78929-195-7 in hardback print format
ISBN: 978-1-78929-306-7 in ebook format

1 2 3 4 5 6 7 8 9 10

The author and publishers have endeavoured to verify
all the facts in this book. Neither the author nor the
publisher can guarantee the accuracy or usability of
any information contained herein, nor accept any
liability for any injury or loss that may occur as a
result of information given in this book.

Designed by Ana Bjezancevic and Barbara Ward
Text by Liz Marvin
Illustrations by Annie Davidson

Printed and bound in Germany

www.mombooks.com

MIX
Papier aus verantwor-
tungsvollen Quellen
FSC® C011124

THE

WINDOWSILL GARDENER

50 Easy-to-grow Plants to Transform your Home

Text by Liz Marvin
Illustrated by Annie Davidson

Michael O'Mara Books Limited

INTRODUCTION

Your home is your garden

You don't need a garden to be a gardener. With a bit of imagination, patience and trial and error, you can fill your windowsills, kitchen counters, bookshelves and more with glorious greenery that you can eat, use to flavour your cooking, brew into a relaxing tea or simply enjoy for what it brings to your home.

The best bit is that you hardly have to spend anything. There are lots of companies online that will send you a whole host of fully grown houseplants apparently perfect for your space, but the truth is that it is easy to grow your own plants from seeds, cuttings and even from kitchen scraps that we would usually throw away. There's no need to buy expensive containers either –

there are plenty of ways you can personalize your plants, such as repurposing tin cans to create a herb garden, making your own hanging baskets or planting **chilli** (see page 97) plants in small coffee sacks.

This book will show you how to green up your home while growing things you can actually eat. Just because you don't have any outdoor space doesn't mean a crop of delicious homegrown **tomatoes** (see page 142) or **baby spinach** (see page 35) is out of reach. Some of the plants in these pages are so easy to grow you can even do so to order – how about a trayful of **microgreens** (see page 26), **pea shoots** (see page 32) or **radishes** (see page 56) ready for your next dinner party?

Whether you're already pretty sure you have a green thumb or you are a complete beginner, have a look through these pages, see what inspires you, grab some compost and make a start. Gardening – indoors or out – is not an exact science; it's all about instinct and the only way to learn is by doing.

Get growing

First things first, what spots do you have in your living space that would be a good home for your garden? Your kitchen is the most obvious for herbs and other edibles, but what about other places, such as bookshelves, coffee tables, hallways – even the stairs. Don't forget that – in spite of the name of this book – so long as they are getting the light they need, plants don't have to just live on windowsills; they can also hang in baskets, stack on work surfaces or sit on the tops of cupboards.

Have a walk around your house and think about where the best growing spots might be. For some plants, a lot of light is non-negotiable – for example, **lavender** (see page 108) and particularly citrus trees, such as **lemon** (see page 151) and **dwarf mandarin** (see page 148) – whereas others, such as **ferns** (see page 80) or **bean sprouts** (see page 38), need far less. Some plants are very happy somewhere with a lot of humidity, but others will struggle. You may find that different places work at different times of the year, too – a warm, sunny windowsill in the spring might become a toaster for your plants by the middle of summer. Sunlight and temperature will be the biggest deciding factors for your plants, so you may find that spring and early autumn are your best growing seasons for edibles.

The best way to find out is just to try. As a lot of the plants covered in this book can be grown from kitchen scraps you would have otherwise thrown away, and you can fashion a plant pot from almost anything (see page 22), the only thing you need to buy is a bit of compost. Experiment with different seedlings and cuttings in different locations at different times of the year. You'll soon get the hang of observing and listening to your plants and you'll be able to tell when they are happy and when they might need a change of scene. And, yes, of course you should talk to them!

Your windowsill family

The plants in these pages have been chosen because you should be able to grow all of them indoors on a sunny windowsill, though they do present different levels of challenge. So if you're a novice it might be best to start with some herbs and some **microgreens** (see page 26) rather than going straight in with **doorstep potatoes** (see page 165) and a **dwarf mandarin tree** (see page 148).

It's usually best to begin with a few cuttings and some seeds and see how you get on. As mentioned above, some spots in your home will be better for growing plants than others – more on this below. As your confidence grows, so can your windowsill family.

Of course, think about what you will actually use, how much space it will take up and how long it will take to grow. If you're going away in a couple of weeks, then there's not much point planting a lot of seeds that will just be coming up and needing watering as you're packing your bags. If you don't like spicy food then there's little point in growing **chillies** (see page 97).

Greening up your home: the basics

In the main, just a bit of patience, a little sunshine and a dash of creativity is all you need to get started. Apart from that, a lot of the plants in this book just need some compost and some care. Although many can be grown for free from cuttings or kitchen scraps in a pot you've repurposed, there are a few extra tools that you will find helpful, particularly as you start to expand your windowsill garden.

 A small watering can with a rose or 'shower' attachment

 A spray mister (when planting seeds and caring for seedlings)

 Scissors, for harvest time

 A thermometer (really handy for knowing how warm different spots in your home are when trying to figure out what might flourish there)

 Potting mix

Soil, glorious soil

Here's a topic that can entertain gardeners for hours. It's true that some fussy plants do need a particular potting mix (and less fussy ones, too – for example, **succulents** (see page 103) require a mix containing lots of sand, or similar, for drainage). But, on the other hand, a good indoor potting compost that is well aerated and will hold on to water can be used for most things, particularly edibles. It is important to get one that's up to the job, though – growing indoors comes with different considerations and getting the right potting mix will make a big difference to the success of your windowsill garden.

Some mixes for indoor gardening don't contain any soil at all – they're based on coir, which is ground-up coconut fibre, with such ingredients as bone meal, peat moss and vermiculite (sometimes perlite) added in. Vermiculite (or perlite) is the little white or light brown specks you see in the mix. It helps the soil stay aerated and retain moisture and is a useful and important ingredient.

Whatever you do, though, don't use soil from outside to pot up your indoor plants, and if you are digging up a plant from outdoors to bring in, get rid of as much of the soil around the roots as you can. Not only is garden soil too heavy and thick for indoor plants, but it is likely to contain bugs and pests that will be very happy to be brought into your home.

TIP: Some plants will really appreciate a dose of fertilizer every so often during the growing season – with **tomatoes** (see page 142), for example, it's pretty much essential to get the most out of your crop. Buy organic if you can – liquid kelp and fish fertilizer is a good general one (if somewhat smelly). You could also try using coffee grounds on your tomatoes and other acid-loving plants. Resist the temptation to over-fertilize, though, as you may 'burn' the roots.

Time for a drink

If you are gardening outside, this would be less of a consideration, but the windowsill gardener needs to water smart. First, where is the water going to go when it drains through the pot at watering time? Ideally, you want a container that has holes in the bottom inside another container that doesn't. This lessens the consequences of accidental overwatering, meaning the plant doesn't sit in wet soil for a long time, which can result in rot and sad, yellow leaves. But when that water does drain through you need something to catch it, so you don't get soil and water all over your lovely windowsill, table or bookshelf.

A container with holes in also gives you the option to water from the bottom by briefly immersing the lower part of the pot in a sink full of water, letting it soak up into the soil. This can be a really handy technique for watering delicate shoots and seedlings.

If you have an amazing pot that you can't make holes in or rest another pot inside, it's still often worth a shot.

Some fine gravel or even charcoal in the bottom can provide space for drainage and aid aeration. If it's not happening, you'll know for next time.

The best time to water is in the morning or the evening as plants generally don't want their wet leaves exposed to direct sun. Seedlings tend to flourish best in a more humid environment and enjoy misting (established plants will appreciate this, too, if the weather is very warm and dry); a tray of almost-there **rocket/arugula** (see page 62), for example, will like to be gently watered from above from a watering can with a rose attachment so as not to upset the roots, and full-grown plants and herbs usually like to have only their roots watered.

Get to know your plants

There is an indication for each plant in this book as
to how much water it requires, but don't forget that it
can depend on a lot of other factors, such as where the
plant is, how much sun it gets, what time of year it is
(lots of plants require less water in the winter months)
and even what sort of pot it's in – a large plastic
pot will be able to retain more water than a small
terracotta one. Some plants like to dry out completely,
whereas others need regular watering. So the best
thing to do is get to know your plants; look at them
every day and you'll learn how to spot that they are not
happy with the amount of water you are giving them
(and remember that too much can be just as much of a
problem as too little).

We all have the best of intentions to care for our leafy
friends responsibly but it's still easy to occasionally
forget. A good way to remember is to build five minutes
of gardening into your daily routine. How about
walking around the house with a spray mister and a
watering can while you're waiting for your morning

coffee to brew? Or making a point of checking on your charges every evening after dinner? And be careful of putting a pot in an out-of-the-way spot you are likely to forget about – after all, out of sight, out of mind.

PESTS

You don't want to share your windowsill harvest with anyone you haven't invited round, but occasionally it will happen and you'll get a visit from an aphid crew. First, move the plant away from any unaffected neighbours and remove any heavily infected leaves. Then, fill a mister bottle with lukewarm water and a squirt of liquid soap and spray the top and underside of the leaves of the affected plant every day until your unwelcome guests get the message.

Many herbs actually make good insect repellents, too. You can use them before an infestation gets out of hand or to prevent a recurrence. Either fresh or dried, or infused in a tea for spraying, chamomile, chives, coriander/cilantro, dill, fennel, feverfew, garlic, lavender, pennyroyal, rosemary and tansy all drive away pests.

DISEASE

Plants that live inside can be susceptible to mould and fungal infections. Making sure there's enough airflow around them and they are not over-watered is the best way to prevent this. If it happens, move the plant well away from any others and outside for a couple of days if you can. A popular home remedy for mould is to crush a garlic clove into a cup of water, leave it to stand for fifteen minutes and then pour it into your mister bottle to spray on the affected plant.

SPACE TO BREATHE

Just like people, plants need room to breathe. Other than those that you will be harvesting very young – such as with **pea shoots** (see page 32) or **microgreens** (see page 26) – plants that are crammed in too tightly will rarely do well. Most plants also really appreciate a gentle breeze. If it's freezing cold outside you won't want to have all the windows open, but your edibles in particular will need some airflow. As well as causing

mould and mildew, a lack of air often results in rotting seedlings or seeds that aren't germinating. Some edibles usually grown outdoors are actually toughened up by a bit of a crosswind – if your **rainbow chard** (see page 59) is growing up a bit spindly, for example, it might be missing the buffeting around it would get from a good breeze and you could try giving it a couple of hours in a room with a gentle fan.

Pots, pots and more pots

Sure, you can go to your local hardware store or nursery and get lots of brown plastic pots – and purpose-made containers like this do have their uses – but this is where you can get creative. In fact, after filling your home with greenery, some of which you can eat, this is probably the next most fun part of being a windowsill gardener. There are two main practical considerations when choosing a home for your plants: drainage (which we've talked about above) and depth. Some plants that are still suitable for indoor growing have a fairly long central or 'tap' root and will need some depth (we're looking at you, **fennel** – see page 127). Others, such as **microgreens** (see page 26), need but a few centimetres (an inch). But, other than that, get ready to use your imagination!

🌿 Start by looking around your kitchen – what do you have that you're not using? For example, pretty glasses and jars are great for starting cuttings and regrowing **celery** (see page 47) and **lettuce** (see page 53), and a big roasting tin could be repurposed as a tray for **pea shoots** (see page 32).

🌿 Why not check out the local goodwill or charity shop? Old copper pans, unusual jugs and even metal buckets can become eye-catching containers.

🌿 Start thinking twice before you throw anything away. Plastic food trays can be perfect for starting off seedlings and tin cans with the label removed look great with herbs planted in them. Cut the bottom off a drinks bottle and punch holes in the base to make a recycled plant pot. This can then be hidden in a tea pot or other ceramic pot without drainage holes.

🍃 If you know anyone who works in a restaurant, ask them if they can get their hands on any cool containers. Olive oil cans often carry an attractive, distinctive design and catering-sized tins can be a good home for a larger plant, such as an **avocado** tree (see page 130). You can use a metal punch or screwdriver and a hammer to make drainage holes. **Chilli** (see page 97) plants look great growing in small coffee bags.

🍃 Want your plants to perfectly match your décor? Next time you're at the DIY store, grab some terracotta pots and some paint samples. You could even use masking tape and a couple of different colours to create your own two-tone designs. (Make sure you only paint the outside of the pot – and this is best used only for pots housing plants you aren't going to eat, as the paint chemicals could get into the soil.)

🍃 And it's not just pots that can be recycled from things you have at home – an empty spray bottle (that contained something non-toxic, such as olive oil) can be thoroughly cleaned to become a mister and a clear plastic bag is the perfect greenhouse hack if your shoots are struggling to germinate in some dry or chilly air.

HOMEMADE POTS FOR BABY PLANTS

Some plants can be grown easily from seed indoors but don't really like being handled too much. If you plant them in a biodegradable pot they are easy to 'pot up' without disturbing their roots when they reach a size where they need a bigger home – **chillies** (see page 97) and **coriander/cilantro** (see page 124) are examples of this. One method is to plant a seed or two in an eggshell filled with compost. They look really cute sitting in an egg box and the shell can just be squashed and cracked slightly when the time comes to pot up. Alternatively, to make a pot from newspaper:

- Take a full sheet of black and white newspaper. (Coloured print is best avoided due to the chemicals in the ink.)

- Fold the paper to form a long, narrow strip.

- Lay a small cylindrical glass about half the width of the paper on its side on one end of the strip, then roll the paper around the jar, tucking the overhanging edge into the open end of the glass. Don't worry about making it neat.

🌿 Squash and crumple the paper around the glass until the shape feels fairly secure, then slide out the glass.

🌿 Turn the glass around and push the bottom into the newspaper cup to squash and flatten its folded base.

🌿 Pull out the glass and fill the paper with compost – this will help it hold its shape. Stand it in a dish to give it some support when you plant your seeds.

🌿 When your seedling is big enough, just pop the whole thing in a pot of compost and plant as normal. The newspaper will quickly break down and your seedling's delicate roots will be undisturbed.

TIP: This might sound obvious, but any chemicals in the soil, container or in any fertilizers you add to your plants can get into the leaves. You'll no doubt want your windowsill garden to be as natural and organic as possible, so it's worth keeping this in mind.

THE
HOUSEPLANTS

MICROGREENS

Skill level	Time	Light	Water
Very easy	Very quick	Good	Gently, often

These trendy green garnishes and salad ingredients are popular with chefs and home cooks for their concentrated delicious fresh flavours and because they look great, too. Not only do they taste amazing, they are highly nutritious. Studies have shown that they have many times the nutrients packed in their little leaves than in the same amount of the mature plant – maybe even forty times as much.

Microgreens are often expensive to buy ready-grown but perfect for growing indoors. In fact, they generally do better inside than in a garden and they grow super quickly, too – typically from two to four weeks from sowing to harvest. Microgreens are a great place to start if you are new to windowsill gardening, not least because, as they give results so quickly, they will help you identify the best spots in your house for growing.

The best container for growing microgreens is a shallow tray with drainage – any old food container you can punch holes in will work fine. You only need a shallow layer of soil, which should be pre-watered so it's damp but not wringing wet. Don't push it down too much – it needs to be quite light and fluffy (if it's falling through the holes in your container, put some kitchen towel or similar in the bottom). Spread the seeds thickly over the top – much more so than if you were growing the plants to maturity. You really can get a lot of leaves out of a small space. Drape a cloth over them to keep the light out until the seedlings start to come through – generally three or four days later.

Once the seeds germinate, water every day. To avoid flattening them when doing so, especially when they are nearly big enough to pick, stand the tray in a little water in the kitchen sink for a few minutes so it can soak up the water through the drainage holes. Or, alternatively, mist enthusiastically from above. To harvest, when they reach the size you want, simply take a pair of scissors to them. Once you've trimmed them, you may get a second harvest if there are tiny seedlings that need some space, or you might prefer to just start again on your next crop. You can store microgreens in the fridge for a few days if you want to, but it's so much better to cut them as and when you need them, so you eat them while they are utterly fresh.

There are lots of different types of microgreens to try. Five of the most popular ones are featured below, but – warning! – once you start it's easy to get hooked on these magical little leaves and you'll want to experiment with all sorts of different things.

TIP: Create your own mini microgreen garden in an old muffin tin. Just add some fine gravel to the bottom of each hole and then fill with soil. It looks great if you pick a few different sorts of microgreens in contrasting colours.

BROCCOLI

With a delicate flavour and pleasing crunch, baby broccoli greens are also super high in such nutrients as vitamins A and C. Sow the seeds thickly and cut when the 'true leaves' have emerged. They are round and look a little like cress – not, unfortunately, like tiny broccoli florets. That would be cool.

CHARD

If you go for ruby red chard then you get the added bonus of jolly red stalks clustering in your microgreens container. Chard microgreens have a subtle, earthy taste and pack less of a punch than other plants, so this might be a good choice as part of a microgreen mix, when you don't want *all* of your leaves to be a teeny tiny flavour bomb.

PURPLE BASIL

These greens are not holding back – they will sock you with a hit of pure, fragrant, herby goodness, as well as being an appealing deep purple, almost black in colour. Basil looks and tastes great scattered

over a risotto, pasta dish or mozzarella and
tomato salad. It is a fast grower, too – use
the leaves when they are quite small, often
only ten days after germination.

BEETROOT

This classic microgreen looks lovely when
growing, with its deep crimson stems. It
does take a little longer though, as you want
the leaves to be a bit bigger compared to
some other baby greens. Usually this will
be from three weeks to a month. As they
are more substantial, the leaves are great in
salads.

KALE

Kale is one of the most nutrient-packed
veggies on the planet, but you could say
that micro kale is even better, as each leaf
contains four times the high amounts of
vitamins and minerals found in the adult
plant. It's fast to grow, too – you can eat it
when just the first leaves have formed.

PEA SHOOTS

Skill level	Time	Light	Water
Very easy	Very quick	Good	Gently, often

Does anything taste of spring quite like fresh pea shoots? They are also very good for you, containing folate, antioxidants and vitamin C, among other goodies. They are a very easy and undemanding crop and if you have a reasonably sunny spot on your windowsill you can even start them off in the depths of winter. Plus they cost hardly anything to grow!

Just take some dried peas bought from the pulses section of your local grocery store and soak them overnight. Then take a shallow tray of some kind that allows for drainage. Add a thin layer of compost, spritz it with water and then scatter the pea seeds on top. Don't be afraid to crowd them in – they need much less space than plants you're hoping to grow to maturity. Now scatter another thin layer of compost over the top and give that a spritz, too.

The trick is to keep your peas slightly damp but not to overwater them. Depending on how dry the air in your house is, you can do that with your trusty spray mister or by watering from the bottom – so putting the tray into a larger tray of water and allowing it to soak up into the compost.

With a bit of luck you'll have a pea shoot crop in as little as two weeks, though you can let them carry on until they are larger. Just bear in mind that if they get too big they will start to become a little tough and bitter. If you harvest the bigger shoots by snipping them off with kitchen scissors you may well get a second crop as the little ones find themselves with space to grow through.

> **TIP:** Some gardeners think that fruit crates salvaged from market stalls make for great pea shoot trays. You may need to line the bottom with a couple of sheets of newspaper to stop the compost falling through, but they will look great on a countertop.

BABY SPINACH

Skill level	Time	Light	Water
Easy	Very quick	Bright	Regularly

The small size of baby-leaf spinach means it is particularly suited to growing on a windowsill. It's also a multi-talented green, as you can of course put it in a salad raw or add handfuls to all sorts of dishes, from risottos to curries to Greek spinach and feta pie. Plus it's rich in vitamins A, C and K, magnesium and iron.

If you have a larger tray – for example, you could use the one that housed your pea shoots (see page 32) when they've finished – that would mean you could get a decent crop, but really, this undemanding veg doesn't ask much. Even just 10 cms (4 inches) of standard compost should be enough. Spinach prefers cooler weather, so it's a good one to start off in early spring. Water the compost before you plant and allow it to drain, so it's damp but not flooded. Use a chopstick or your finger to make holes about 2.5 cms (1 inch) deep and 10 cms (4 inches) apart. Put two or three seeds in each one. Cover over and mist the soil.

Check every day to see if it needs watering, but only give it a sprinkle when it needs it. Spinach doesn't want to stay wet all the time. You should start to see germination in about a week to two weeks and, depending on the time of year, your crop should be ready for the first harvest a week or two after that. Baby spinach can be harvested any time from when it looks like it's worth eating. Snip near the roots, taking leaves from the outer parts of the plant, as and when you need them.

BEAN SPROUTS

Skill level	Time	Light	Water
Easy	Very quick	Low	Every day

You know that bag of dried mung beans you've got lurking in the back of the cupboard? Well, rather than wasting your money on a supermarket pack of bean sprouts, half of which you didn't actually want and ends up turning to mush in the bottom of the fridge, grow your own ready for your next delicious stir fry. Lentils work well, too, as do chick peas and most pulses that come whole. Health food stores sell packs of 'sprouting mix', containing a variety, all ready to go. Just make sure you use something designed for eating, rather than seeds for planting out.

First of all, rinse your beans, peas or lentils in a sieve with plenty of water. Then, transfer them into a big jar. You'll need something pretty large, and it should be about six times the size of the amount of beans you want to sprout (it's amazing the amount of bean sprouts you get from just a handful of mung beans!).

If you have a jar with a mesh lid then that's perfect, but a muslin cloth and an elastic band will work just as well. Fill the jar almost up to the top with water and leave it in a cool, shady spot in your kitchen overnight. The next day, strain the water out of the jar (this is why the mesh is handy), give it a rinse and drain it again. Then put it back in its spot, lying it on its side.

In about two days' time you will hopefully already have some sprouts. At this point, fill the jar back up with water, give it a good stir and drain the water out. If you can remember, do this once more that day and pop the jar back on its side.

By day four, your sprouts should be ready to go, though you can give them another couple of days if you want them to be longer. Put them in a big bowl of water so the empty bean shells float to the top, and discard them. Now dry the sprouts on some kitchen towel and pick out any beans you can spot that haven't sprouted. They will keep in the fridge for up to six days before they start to go brown and mushy. If they look as if they are drying out, just give them a rinse under the tap.

BUCKWHEAT LETTUCE

Skill level	Time	Light	Water
Easy	Very quick	Bright	Regularly

If your local health food store can sell you some buckwheat groats, why not try this easy, unusual, fast-growing green? No doubt you have heard of buckwheat before – in flour form it is used in all sorts of foods, from Japanese soba noodles to Russian blinis and French galettes. Though it's not actually a wheat at all – it's related to sorrel and rhubarb.

Little buckwheat plants have two round leaves opposite each other and are ready for harvesting when they are about 8-9 cms (3-3.5 inches) tall. This should take less than two weeks from sowing, so they are a brilliant fast crop. They have a delicate and mild flavour and are great in any salad where you don't want a strong taste. They contain vitamins A, B2 and B3, C and also rutin, which can help strengthen blood vessels. Why not chuck a handful into your next green smoothie?

The method is pretty similar to that of growing pea shoots (see page 32), but you don't need quite such a big container (though it will definitely need holes in the bottom). Soak your groats in half a jar of water overnight (or for at least eight hours). Spread over a thin layer of ready-watered compost and scatter a little more compost over the top. You can plant buckwheat groats fairly densely – if you get any fuzziness or rot then they are probably lacking in air circulation. Just pull a few out and put them next to an open window or outside where they can get a bit of a draught.

Harvest your crop all in one go with kitchen scissors and store in the fridge. Sometimes you'll find you get a second crop, so you could try leaving the left-behind bare stalks in the sunshine to see if anything happens.

CARROT TOPS

Skill level	Time	Light	Water
Easy	Quick	Bright	Often

This is a great demonstration of how we can recycle food scraps that we would usually throw away to produce another round of nutritious food – completely for free. In this case, the tops you've trimmed off some store-bought carrots will quickly provide you with some delicious, carroty greenery.

When preparing your carrots, just trim a little bit extra than you usually would off the top, as the new roots will grow out of the side, rather than the bottom – 2.5 cms (1 inch) should be enough. Now put these cut-side down into a saucer of water or into a pot of well-watered compost. The water or compost only needs to come halfway up the side. Place them in a sunny spot and remember to replace the water every few days.

In just a couple of weeks (depending on the time of year) you should start to see some feathery greenery emerge. This underrated leaf is a great source of vitamins, and it has a fresh flavour a bit like parsley (see page 91) and, unsurprisingly, carrots! Use your fluffy carrot tops as you would any herby, leafy green. How about scattering them over some roasted carrots, adding them to a tabbouleh or any similar salad? They go really well with mint (see page 68).

Carrot tops are great to grow with children as they are so easy to plant and yield quick results. You could put some in compost and some in water and race them to compare the results.

CELERY

Skill level	Time	Light	Water
Easy	Quick	Bright	Often

The principle here is pretty much the same as with lettuce (see page 53). Just remember to cut your celery sticks off the bunch, leaving at least 3 cms (just over 1 inch) on the roots. Then, pop the roots into a shallow dish of water, cut end up, and watch the celery magically regrow. When you've got some decent new leaves, plant it in a pot with some compost.

You'll end up with a much leafier plant, rather than celery sticks, but that's OK: celery leaves are pretty special in their own right. They contain the antioxidant vitamin E as well as a decent dose of calcium, among other things. Once your recycled celery plant is looking established and healthy, you can trim a few leaves off to add to your morning smoothie, lunchtime salad or when you're next making soup. In fact, you can use a handful of chopped celery leaves in the same way as you'd use any herb.

One of the tastiest ways of using your celery leaves is in a pesto. In a food processor, blitz a couple of garlic cloves, then add three or four handfuls of celery leaves and a small handful of nuts – pine nuts, cashews or almonds will all work well. Blend them together, scraping the mixture back down the bowl towards the blades as you need to. Add a good glug of olive oil and finally a couple of spoonfuls of grated parmesan. It will keep in a jar in the fridge for about a week – except you'll eat it before then as it goes with almost anything!

GARLIC GREENS

Skill level	Time	Light	Water
Easy	Quick	Medium–bright	Regularly

You know those smaller, annoying cloves you always get in a bulb of garlic that are really fiddly to peel? Hang on to them and poke them into a pot of compost, pointy end just below the surface, about 2.5 cms (1 inch) apart. In a couple of weeks the bulbs will sprout and start growing long green shoots. Once they get to a decent length, trim the ends off with kitchen scissors. Leave a good few centimetres (an inch or so) behind so as not to shock the plant too much and they will happily grow back. As the cloves start to get bigger and crowd the pot, you can pull them out and use the whole thing.

The flavour of garlic greens is a little like wild garlic, but less pungent and not so earthy. You can use them as a garlicky version of chives – add them to any dish in the same way you would another strong-tasting green herb. You could try scattering some sliced garlic greens across a piece of white fish, wrapping it up in baking paper with some slices of lemon and baking the whole thing in the oven. Or, even better, make your own garlic butter by mixing a few spoonfuls of garlic greens chopped as finely as you can into some good butter with salt and pepper. It'll be a lovely jazzy green colour plus, this way, you won't get off-putting chunks of raw garlic in your garlic bread or on your steak.

LETTUCE

Skill level	Time	Light	Water
Easy	Quick	Bright	Often

Don't throw the end of that lettuce away! With almost no effort you can use it to grow a whole new lettuce.

All you need to do is put it in a glass or dish of water on a sunny (but not too bright) windowsill. The key is to keep the end of the lettuce touching the water without submerging the whole thing so it rots. You'll need to keep the water topped up and you might want to change it occasionally if it starts to go green – although using small teacups or coloured glasses can improve the general look here.

Within a week or so, you should start to see signs that your lettuce is regrowing. At this point, you could put it in a pot with some compost to prolong its life and encourage it to grow bigger, perhaps pulling off a few leaves at a time as you need them. Or when it seems like they won't get any bigger., you could save yourself the trouble and use all the new leaves. Either way, you'll be giving a food waste-bound scrap a whole new lease of life as a productive and tasty member of your windowsill garden in return for just seconds of your time.

Note that this won't work for all types of lettuce – cos, romaine and similar types of compact, oval-shaped lettuces are the best for this, but it's so easy to do that it's worth having a go with any kind that has a decent, firm stem. After all, if it doesn't happen, you can just chuck it in the compost, where it was headed anyway!

RADISHES

Skill level	Time	Light	Water
Easy	Quick	Bright	Often

Radishes are a great crop to get started early in the spring. Most varieties are surprisingly quick to grow, you can eat the leaves as well as the root and, when homegrown, they have a distinctive taste that just can't be matched by something that has been hanging around in a grocery store for a few days.

Poke your radish seeds about a centimetre (an inch) down into a pot of pre-watered indoor potting mix, about 5 cms (2 inches) apart, and sprinkle a light dusting of soil over the top, giving it a quick mist. If it's early in the year, covering the pot with a clear plastic bag to keep the seeds snug and damp until they germinate will speed things up.

Once the seedlings are underway, keep them well-watered, without drowning them, of course. You will probably need to thin the seedlings out as they get bigger, but don't throw the weaker ones away – after a quick rinse they'll be a delicious addition to any salad.

Harvest your radishes when they are still quite young and tender. Left too long and they can get a bit woody. With a bit of luck, you could have jewel-like, juicy, peppery radishes in not much more than a month after sowing.

RAINBOW CHARD

Skill level	Time	Light	Water
Easy	Medium	Medium	Regularly

Chard is highly nutritious, easy and fairly speedy to grow, can be eaten raw or cooked and, with its jaunty, brightly coloured stems, it looks great, too. Plus, if you plant some chard seeds in late summer, you'll have a lovely crop of bright green leaves just as the weather is turning darker and green things feel in shorter supply.

Chard doesn't need a very deep pot but bear in mind that its leaves are going to be fairly sizable, so it will need stability if you don't want to be righting a stricken pot too often. Sow a few seeds into well-watered soil, then cover with a light dusting of compost and mist. If it feels like they are taking ages to germinate, and you think it might be because your house is a bit chilly, try securing a clear plastic bag over the top with an elastic band to create a makeshift greenhouse.

Baby leaves look stunning in a salad, whereas larger chard can be treated as if it is an overdressed kale or flamboyant spinach. A top chef tip is to cut the stalks away from the leaves and cook them slightly differently. The stems will take a little longer to become tender, so they can be gently sautéed in butter or olive oil before adding the shredded leaves at the end and allowing them to wilt down. Chard's robust nutty, earthy flavours make it a perfect teammate to cream cheese and smoked fish.

TIP: A trick to help germination is to soak the seeds in lukewarm water for a couple of hours before you plant them.

ROCKET/ARUGULA

Skill level	Time	Light	Water
Easy	Quick	Medium	Regularly, gently

If you have enough space on your windowsill for a long, narrow or square tray, at least 12 cms (roughly 4.5 inches) deep, rocket/arugula is a great one to try. It has a delicious, spicy, peppery taste and grows best in the cooler months, so you can plant it in autumn and early spring. Depending on the time of year, it may only be a couple of weeks from sowing the seeds to adding the leaves to your salad.

Prepare your tray with a layer of compost – the deeper this is the bigger your leaves can grow. Scatter the seeds and sprinkle a thin, fine layer of compost over the top. Water it gently and well. If you are sowing your rocket early in the year, you could secure a clear plastic bag over the top to keep the seeds warm. Once they've sprouted, you can use any seeds you have left to fill in the gaps.

When the leaves have grown large enough to eat, start harvesting the bigger ones with kitchen scissors, leaving the little ones to grow through. The flavour of the bigger leaves will be fairly punchy, while the smaller ones will have a more delicate taste. The leaves you've cut will mostly regrow and you should get about three shots at this before they get straggly and rather too bitter.

Make sure you give your rocket enough water – without drowning it, of course. If it gets too hot it is very prone to bolting – this is plant-speak for it suddenly developing flowers and going to seed. You can eat the flowers, but your crop will get rather tough and be more stem than leaf. To avoid this, if the weather turns warm, move the tray to a shady windowsill, even putting it outside if you have the space. And if the weather turns cold, keep it away from radiators and other heat sources. You might feel cosy but your rocket plants will feel sad.

CHIVES

Skill level	Time	Light	Water
Easy	Quick	Bright	Regularly

The smallest and most delicate of the onion family, chives pack much more of a punch than their slim build suggests. They go really well with potato and egg – try adding chopped chives to a creamy, summery new potato salad. The advantage of growing your own chives on a windowsill is that you can help yourself when you like, rather than having to buy a whole cut bunch in a plastic bag, inevitably finding they're a bit battered and bruised by the time you get them home.

You can easily grow chives from seed, starting in late winter. To harvest your chives, trim out the longest stalks close to the base. This will stop them getting straggly and encourage the plant to produce more stalks. It's a good idea to do this even if you're not planning to use the stalk – you can always chop them and put them in an ice cube tray with some water, then freeze, ready to use another day.

Chives are one of the few herbs that we don't mind if they flower (rosemary and thyme are others; see pages 71 and 118). Chive flowers are purple, or slightly pinky. They are tasty and make a pretty salad garnish. Just make sure you trim the flowers from the plant before they start to wilt, as it will help keep your chive plant bushy and productive.

MINT

Skill level	Time	Light	Water
Easy	Medium	Bright	Regularly

M int is thought to aid concentration, so if you ever work from home you might benefit from keeping a mint plant close at hand. Next time you buy some mint sprigs for cooking with, or if you have access to an established mint plant you can take cuttings from, strip off the lower leaves from a few sprigs and put them in a glass of water to grow some roots. Don't overcrowd them – the leaves need access to sunlight to help the stems grow roots. It might be best to put them in individual glasses. Once they have about three roots a couple of centimetres (an inch) long, you can plant them up in a pot. It's fine to put a few cuttings in the same pot.

Mint plants like to live somewhere with a reasonable amount of sunlight, so long as it's not baking hot. They prefer regular watering, but don't want to be absolutely saturated the whole time. You might find you need to rotate them every few days as they tend to grow towards the light source and may get rather straggly. As with basil (see page 121), it's a good idea to pinch out the tops if this happens, to encourage them to grow more bushy.

Once your mint is established, harvest a few stems at a time to add to your cooking, use in a cup of calming mint tea, or pop in an even more calming mojito.

A NOTE OF CAUTION: Mint doesn't play well with others. Don't be tempted to combine it with other herbs in one pot: overbearing mint will soon take over.

ROSEMARY

Skill level	Time	Light	Water
Easy	Medium	Medium	Occasionally

You only need a few sprigs of rosemary to add something extra to lamb dishes, roast potatoes and even meaty pasta dishes, such as lasagne. It's super easy to grow a rosemary plant from a cutting and much better than trying to grow from seed, as it can take ages to get going. You probably know someone with a rosemary bush in their garden (or keep your eyes out for one overhanging the footpath in a residential street that could be fair game!).

To take a cutting, snip off four or five stems about 10 cms (4 inches) long from the plant. Carefully slice off the lower leaves and pop the cuttings in a jam jar on the windowsill with water that shouldn't reach the bottom leaves. Once your cuttings have grown about three decent roots, plant them up around the edge of a small pot of compost. Just make sure your pot has a hole in the bottom for good drainage. Rosemary doesn't really like to sit in soggy soil.

When planted outdoors, this evergreen can grow to be almost shrub-sized, usually with pale blue or sometimes pinky-purple flowers. The health benefits of rosemary are thought to include anti-inflammatory properties and it may even help to lower blood-sugar levels. Some people find rosemary tea helps them feel less anxious or stressed. In the language of flowers, rosemary stands for remembrance, so, at the very least, maybe a pot of rosemary on your windowsill will remind you to water all your other plants.

TIP: Once you've got your rosemary plant established, why not plant it up in an old tea caddy? This is a great way to reuse unwanted items lying around your home and it will look very stylish.

PLANTS TO BOOST
YOUR WELLBEING

In the past few years we've seen a renewed interest in houseplants. Perhaps because we've become more aware of the calming effect of bringing a little bit of nature into our living spaces – or maybe because we've seen how great they can make a room look on Instagram! It doesn't really matter what the reason is, though; we all know from personal experience that being in a space with lots of greenery makes us feel better. Here are three inexpensive (or free) houseplants that most people will find easy to fit into their space and look after, which come with some extra benefits.

ENGLISH IVY

Skill level	Time	Light	Water
Easy	Medium	Medium–bright	Regularly

This very common plant is so easy to grow – all you have to do is find a plant you like the look of and trim off a few cuttings. Remove the bottom leaves and place the stems in a glass of water. They'll soon take root and you can pot them up. Ivy will grow happily even in a fairly shady corner and it usually won't hold it against you if you forget the occasional watering. It looks stunning trailing down from a high shelf or hanging pot. Some studies have shown that ivy can remove the pollutant formaldehyde from the air and it is thought to combat mould particles, too. Plus, in ancient European cultures, ivy was thought to drive out evil spirits, and you never know when that might come in handy.

SNAKE PLANT

Skill level	Time	Light	Water
Easy	Medium	Medium–low	When dry

While ivy romantically drapes itself over anything nearby, a snake plant is all about strong lines and upward energy. It can grow to 2 metres (over 6 feet) tall but will probably reach a maximum of 90 cms (about 3 feet) in a pot. The snake plant doesn't mind low light levels and it only needs watering every couple of months in the winter. A plant that is growing too big for its pot can be split by dividing its rhizome – or subterranean stem/root system – and repotting in two different pots. Snake plants are one of the very few plants to release oxygen at night, and they have been shown to have the ability to remove such toxins as benzene and formaldehyde from the air. (They are mildly toxic to dogs and cats if eaten, though, so keep out of the way of nibbly pets.)

BOSTON FERN

Skill level	Time	Light	Water
Easy	Medium	Low–medium	When dry

The Victorians were big fans of a Boston fern and there's certainly something about this big ball of frothy greenery that will make you feel more relaxed, even if your corset is done up a little too tight. Similar to most ferns, this plant originates from humid climes and absorbs moisture from the air. So it's a great plant for a bathroom, where it will help take up a bit of the humidity and will put up with the sort of dim, steamy conditions that would cause an affront to most other plants. Boston ferns also come high up the list in studies into which plants are able to remove pollutants from the air.

CHERVIL

Skill level	Time	Light	Water
Fairly easy	Medium	Medium–low	Regularly

Much overlooked, chervil is the elegant and sophisticated yet delicate cousin to the more robust and workaday parsley (see page 91). It is one of the herbs that makes up the classic French *fines herbes* mix, along with parsley, tarragon and chives (see page 65).

Grow chervil from seed by sowing directly into the pot that you want it to live in (it doesn't like to be transplanted). Do ensure that you keep the soil moist but not soggy, and it shouldn't take more than about eight weeks before it's ready to harvest. In the meantime, you can thin out the seedlings as they come through to ensure that the pot won't be too crowded and add these to your cooking. Another great thing about chervil is that it doesn't mind lower light levels, so it's a good one for a shadier corner of the kitchen bench.

As with coriander/cilantro (see page 124) it will not live that long and it doesn't like to get too hot, so don't feel like a failure if your chervil starts to die back after a few months. While it's thriving, make the most of it by scattering it over fish, courgettes, mushrooms fried in butter or stir it through scrambled eggs.

TIP: Chervil loses its flavour when heated, so always sprinkle it over a dish that has finished cooking.

LEMONGRASS

Skill level	Time	Light	Water
Fairly easy	Medium	Medium–bright	Regularly

This delicious, fragrant native of Asia and Africa really is a grass. Away from its home, it's often sold in sad little plastic packets and it's not cheap, either. But if you can visit an Asian market and get your hands on a bunch with the root end just about intact, you'll find it's surprisingly easy to grow your own lemongrass plants.

Strip off any outside leaves that look past their best, exposing the lower bulb. Chop the tops off to leave yourself about 8 cms (just over 3 inches) above the roots. Put them in a glass with a few centimetres (an inch) of water in the bottom. Kept somewhere light, but not in intense direct sunlight, they should start to grow roots quite quickly.

Push your fledgling plants into some damp compost a few centimetres (an inch) apart. You can start them in a small pot to see how they get on, but once they get established and the roots start to show through the bottom of the pot, you may need to upsize their home. When grown outdoors, lemongrass can reach up to 1.5 metres (5 feet) in height, so you may need to keep an eye on it. When your plants are established, you can harvest a whole stem by cutting it off at soil level or trim the grassy leaves to use in cooking or to make a refreshing tea.

TIP: Lemongrass makes a delicious syrup for use in cocktails. Heat a cup of sugar and a cup of water together in a pan, stirring until the sugar is dissolved. Drop in a tablespoonful of sliced lemongrass and allow it to infuse for a couple of hours before straining. Try it with vodka or white rum and soda. Delicious!

OREGANO

Skill level	Time	Light	Water
Fairly easy	Medium	Bright	When dry

O regano looks like a cross between basil (see page 121) and thyme (see page 118) and tastes a bit like it, too. It's often left out of tomato-based dishes in favour of bigger and flashier basil. Overlook oregano no longer! A staple of Greek and Mexican cuisine, some love it as its flavour holds its own alongside other strong-tasting ingredients, particularly hot chilli and sour feta. Its Mediterranean background means it's a tough and resilient plant that thrives in hot, dry conditions.

Oregano is easy to grow indoors. Grow it from seed from late winter onwards. Sow the seeds into a tray filled with damp compost and scatter some fine compost over the top. Fixing a clear plastic bag or sheet over the top will help keep the seeds warm and encourage them to germinate. Small established seedlings can be transferred into large pots – any that you don't want or don't look like they will make it can be rinsed and put straight into your dinner.

In terms of watering, as with lots of Mediterranean plants, oregano would choose little and often – if it is kept too wet its roots will rot. Keep picking sprigs of oregano to keep your plant in a good orderly shape. If it flowers, give it a good trim once it's finished. Indoors, your oregano plant should last through the winter. Just trim any dead stems away at the base.

PARSLEY

Skill level	Time	Light	Water
Fairly easy	Medium	Medium	Regularly

All herbs are better cut fresh from your very own windowsill garden, of course, but fresh parsley in particular really is streets ahead of potpourri-tasting dried flakes. The two most common types are curly – with its scrumpled-up leaves – and the stronger flavoured flat-leaf or continental parsley.

Lots of big grocery stores sell 'living' parsley plants to take home and cook with. As with basil, if you split it up into two separate plants and trim it back a bit, it is often possible to create two flourishing plants. Or, if you have bought a packet of cut parsley it's worth popping a few sprigs into a glass of water to see if they will take root. You might get lucky. The deciding factor is whether the leaves wilt before the roots appear.

You can also grow parsley from seed in a tray of compost in good light. Sow the seeds about a centimetre (an inch) deep and 4-5 cms (1.5-2 inches) apart. Parsley has a longer germination time than other herbs, so don't be alarmed if it's taking a while. Although, having said that, in medieval times it was thought that the seeds took so long to sprout because they had to travel to hell and back seven times first. So perhaps be a *bit* alarmed.

TIP: If you can get your hands on an old-fashioned milk carton – the kind that opens all the way up at the top – this would be an eye-catching home for your parsley. Just add some gravel to the bottom to help drainage and then fill with compost, up to about 4 cms (1.5 inches) or so from the top, before carefully planting your parsley plant.

SAGE

Skill level	Time	Light	Water
Fairly easy	Medium, some patience	Bright	When dry

With its elegant silvery, oval leaves, common sage earns its place in a windowsill herb garden on aesthetics alone, though its rich, slightly piney taste means it will also add a delicious twist to your cooking, for which you'll only need to grab a few leaves at a time. Add it to potato dishes or place a few sprigs inside a chicken before you roast it. It's also fabulous in autumnal squash dishes. Sage is thought to have many health benefits, too. Similar to rosemary (see page 71), it contains rosmarinic acid, an antioxidant that studies have shown can relieve inflammation.

To grow sage from a cutting, you'll need a sprig that's at least 10 cms (4 inches) long. Remove the leaves from the lower half and poke it into a small pot of some ready-watered compost. If the bottom leaves turn yellow after a couple of weeks, don't worry, just snip them off. It's likely a sign that the roots are growing.

Sage is fairly tolerant of inexperienced and forgetful gardeners – once established, a rather dried-out plant can usually be brought back to life with a good watering. It will need a sunny spot and you might need to wait until the plant is established before you start snipping at it too enthusiastically.

Some people believe that wafting burning bunches of dried herbs can cleanse a space of negative energy. Just make sure you turn off the smoke alarm first ...

TIP: Sage tea is thought to relieve upset stomachs and calm sore throats. Grate some lemon rind over a couple of handfuls of sage leaves in a jug. Pour in boiling water, cover with a lid or plate, and allow to steep for about twenty minutes. Stir in some honey and either reheat or serve cold over ice.

CHILLIES

Skill level	Time	Light	Water
Easy	Medium	Full	When dry

Chillies might just be the perfect indoor plants. They don't need much space and they are happy on a windowsill, where the fruits will bring you a cheery flash of colour. Plus, you only need a fruit or two from them at a time to add a bit of fire to your cooking.

There are hundreds of varieties of chilli plants, from blow-your-socks-off hot to is-this-really-a-chilli mild. They are best grown from seed and it's worth doing a bit of research to choose the best plants for what you want. For example, the popular variety 'Demon Red' is compact, well-suited to windowsills and produces cute little red chillies that pack a punch. Whereas the small 'NuMex Twilight' chillies change colour from purple to yellow to orange to red, producing an eye-catching display.

Late winter is a good time to plant. Follow the packet instructions and fashion your own propagator simply by placing the seed tray or pots into a clear plastic bag on the windowsill until the little green shoots appear. When they are big enough to handle, you can transfer the seedlings into their own pots (or paper pots – see page 22). Any spare plants will make great gifts.

Yellow dropping leaves is generally a sign that you've been a bit too free with the watering can. Some chilli growers suggest it's best to give your chilli plant a really good dousing once in a while and then leave the soil to dry out before soaking it again.

TIP: The Scoville Scale is used to measure the spiciness of chillies, which is measured in SHUs, or Scoville Heat Units. The very spiciest chillies come in at over 500,000 SHU, meaning they have to be diluted 300,000-fold for their heat to be undetectable. Eek!

MAKRUT (KAFFIR) LIME TREE

Skill level	Time	Light	Water
Easy	Needs patience	Full	Regularly

M akrut lime leaves – *bai ma gruut* in Thai – are a key ingredient in Thai, Indonesian and Cambodian food but, like lemongrass (see page 85), in lots of countries a small packet of these leaves is expensive, and they can be hard to find. It will be much easier to purchase this as a ready-made plant, either from your local grocery store or online.

With a bit of care, a makrut lime tree makes for a great houseplant. It's elegant, fragrant and it doesn't grow too fast so it won't take over. Hopefully, it will fruit and you will get funny, knobbly limes to use in your cooking, but even if it doesn't you'll love having the distinctive double leaves to hand.

Like all citrus trees, makrut limes do like to maintain quite firm boundaries, though they are generally more relaxed than a lemon tree (see page 151). However, you'll still need to make sure you provide well-drained soil and a sunny spot at the very least. Yellowing leaves can be a sign of overwatering, so watch out for this as the roots can rot. Gently prune the tree from time to time to encourage it to grow into a nice bushy shape.

Now you're ready to leap in and discover all the amazing dishes you can create with these fragrant leaves growing in your very own home.

SUCCULENTS

Skill level	Time	Light	Water
Easy	Quick	Bright	With spray mister

'Succulents' is the name for the group of plants that store water in their leaves, allowing them to survive in harsh, dry habitats – such as the bookshelf of a slightly forgetful windowsill gardener! They have become super popular houseplants thanks to the wide array of interesting-looking varieties available and because they are so easy to care for.

Another great thing about succulents is how easy they are to propagate. Many types of succulents will grow from a leaf that has been cut from or fallen off the parent plant. You just need to make sure that it's a complete leaf with the whole stem intact. Ensure you wear gloves and use tongs to gather a few leaves (they can be spiky!) and then leave them to dry on a paper towel until they start to shrivel. Now lay them down flat on a pot of succulent or cactus potting soil and mist them if they start to look like they are drying out.

Within a few weeks you should see little rosettes of new growth start to appear.

When your plants are a little bigger, they'll need to be properly planted in their own container. You should be able to get rid of the original leaf at this point. Because succulents only have a shallow root system and need only misting rather than watering so they can cope without drainage, you can really use your imagination in terms of pots. How about carefully cutting a hole in an old, unwanted book and dropping in a succulent housed in a yoghurt pot? Or glue a magnet to the pot of a small plant to create an interesting display on your fridge door.

TIP: The one thing that succulents really don't like is much water. They will even struggle in a humid environment. So though they look great, terrariums are actually not the best home for succulents. Try ferns instead.

PLANTS WITH
MAGICAL POWERS

$\mathcal{S}$ ome plants are great to have around, not just because they look good or taste nice, but also because they have an extra something to offer. Here are three plants you can grow indoors that have some pretty impressive benefits.

LAVENDER

Skill level	Time	Light	Water
Medium	Medium	Bright–full	When needed

If you have a bright and sunny spot on your bedroom windowsill then why not try a pot of beautiful blue or purple lavender? Important in aromatherapy, its distinctive aroma is thought to make you feel calm and aid sleep. Plus, with a lavender plant to hand you can make like your granny and put a few dried sprigs in a muslin bag into a cupboard or drawer to deter those hungry moths. And mosquitos aren't really fans either.

There are lots of different types of lavender, but ideally you want one that's on the petite side and will live happily in a pot. Either visit your local nursery or take a cutting from an established plant. It is possible to grow lavender from seed but it could take up to a couple of years to get established, particularly indoors, and do you really want to wait that long?

To take a cutting, cut a green but not woody sprig, 8–10 cms (3–4 inches) long, ideally one that hasn't flowered. Try to find a little bump in the stem that indicates a leaf node and cut just below that. As with sage (see page 94), trim the lower leaves away and poke into a pot of damp compost, pressing in firmly. You should be able to fit a few in a pot. Cover with a clear plastic bag for four weeks or so to make the cuttings think they're in a cosy greenhouse. You'll know the roots have developed when you see new growth on the plant. Once this has happened, you can carefully replant your cuttings into individual pots.

CHAMOMILE

Skill level	Time	Light	Water
Medium	Medium	Bright	Regularly

Sow chamomile in mid-spring and, given a sunny spot, in two to three months you'll have some pretty daisy-like flowers you can harvest for a famously relaxing chamomile tea.

Roman chamomile is the most common flowering kind. You can start your seeds off in a seed tray or just scatter them in the pot you eventually want them to grow in. Water the compost beforehand and then just add the lightest of coverings of fine compost over the top, as they don't really like to be in complete darkness. Give the topsoil a little mist for good measure.

Chamomile can get a little bit straggly, or 'leggy' as gardeners like to call it. So, to keep your plant looking bushy and handsome, trim it down a bit occasionally, even when you're not harvesting the flowers.

You can eat the leaves as well as the flowers, though some people find them rather bitter. To prepare the flowers for making chamomile tea, gather the flower heads when the petals are flat. Spread them on a tray in a single layer and allow to dry for 1–2 weeks in a dark, warm place. To make tea, use about a teaspoon of dried chamomile flowers per cup. Place the blooms in a tea infuser, then pour some boiling water over it. Allow to steep for five minutes or so and then drink. Sweet dreams!

ALOE VERA

Skill level	Time	Light	Water
Medium	Medium	Bright	Occasionally

A loe vera is an amazing plant that really earns its place in any home, even the most bijou apartment. Not only do the long, pointed leaves give a structural focal point to any room, the 'gel' contained within them has amazing health benefits, particularly for the skin. The anti-inflammatory gel that oozes out of an aloe leaf has been used as a treatment for wounds and burns for hundreds, even thousands, of years. It's also a gentle and effective treatment for acne and dandruff, and some people add aloe juice to drinks and smoothies to promote gut health.

Aloe is a type of succulent, so if you have any potting mix for succulents this will work well. Otherwise, mix about half-and-half potting mix and sand. If your aloe plant comes in a plastic pot consider repotting it into terracotta, as it will likely prefer this porous material. As it's a desert plant it doesn't like having wet feet, so be careful not to overwater.

It's hard to grow aloe vera from a cutting, but happy plants will often throw out offshoots – rather adorably called 'pups'. If you carefully slide the whole plant out of the pot you should be able to gently separate out the root system of the aloe pup before planting it in its own pot.

To harvest a leaf for use, cut it off near the base of the plant using a sterilized knife (plants can get infections, too). Drain or remove the yellow-ish resin, called the 'aloin', and discard – it's a strong laxative, so make sure you don't eat this! – then slice the leaf down the middle and squeeze out the gel, or peel the whole thing with a vegetable peeler. You can keep the gel in a jar in the fridge for a couple of days. Chilled aloe gel might be the nicest-feeling treatment for sunburn there is.

TIP: Why not try mixing aloe vera with coconut oil to create a hydrating body cream – lather over your hands and feet for a soothing effect after a long day. Or mix with honey to create a sweet and hydrating face mask.

THYME

Skill level	Time	Light	Water
Medium	Medium	Bright	When dry

Perky, aromatic thyme is a member of the mint family and it is used in cuisine all around the world, from France to Jamaica. It's packed with a zingy, savoury flavour (though try a little in cookies and ice cream, too) and a few sprigs go a long way, so it's a perfect addition to your windowsill herb garden. And it has also been shown to help keep the bugs away.

Thyme is a no-nonsense plant that will forgive you if you forget to water it occasionally – in fact, it likes to dry out a bit before a thorough dousing. It does need a fair bit of light but this doesn't all have to be direct sunlight – so it will usually manage on a kitchen countertop. Don't worry if it flowers – it won't really affect the flavour and the flowers can be a beautiful cocktail garnish. There are lots of different types – why not try some lemon thyme, caraway thyme or eye-catching variegated thyme?

Thyme is easy to grow from seed, though it can take a while to germinate. To grow thyme from a cutting, cut sprigs from the plant low down near the roots and strip the leaves from the lower half. Pinch out any flowers. Make some holes in a pot of compost using a pencil or a chopstick and poke the cuttings in. You should be able to get in three or more, depending on the size of the pot. Push the soil in around them and very gently water in. If your house isn't too warm, cut the bottom off a large soft-drink bottle and put it over the cuttings like a mini greenhouse. You should see some signs of growth within about four weeks.

BASIL

Skill level	Time	Light	Water
Medium	Medium	Bright	Regularly

This staple of any herb garden smells amazing, looks lovely and has a whole range of culinary uses – so who wouldn't like a lovely bushy green basil plant or two on their windowsill?

You can grow basil from seed, but if summer is on the way and homemade pizza and pasta sauces are on the horizon, then you might decide you don't have time for this (it can also be tricky to get basil seeds going indoors). It's worth trying a cutting if you buy a bunch of cut basil for cooking with. Or lots of grocery stores sell whole 'living' plants for next to nothing. They are usually grown with too many stems crammed into a small space for the plant to flourish long term, so take it out of its container and gently split it into two or three, replanting them into separate pots. Try to wait until your new basil plants get over the shock of their experiences before you harvest too many leaves.

In order to perform well, basil does have a few things on its wish list. It likes six hours of sun a day, or more, ideally, so you may struggle to get it through a very dark winter. However, it is known as a 'tender annual' – if it's put in powerful, direct sunlight its leaves will toast and it will dry out quickly. So you might need to try your basil plant in a few different locations before deciding on its new home. To harvest basil, take the leaves from the top of the plant. This will encourage the plant to grow thick and leafy rather than tall and straggly. Also, you don't want your basil to flower as this can change the flavour of the leaves.

CORIANDER/CILANTRO

Skill level	Time	Light	Water
Medium	Medium	Bright	When dry

This staple of Asian, South and Central American cooking can be grown indoors, but it is a bit of a diva. It's best grown from seed, as it's hard to get cuttings to root before the leaves wilt and die. It doesn't like to be transplanted, so sow it in paper pots or even eggshells (see page 22) and then you can put the whole thing in the final pot. It will also need very good drainage, feeding with plant food every couple of weeks and watering when the soil becomes dry, but not until then. It will also throw a tantrum and go to seed very quickly if it gets too hot, which changes the flavour.

Once your plant starts to become established, pinch a couple of centimetres (an inch) off the ends of a few stems at a time to encourage it to become bushy. When the plant is big enough you can harvest whole stems by cutting them off at the bottom of the plant.

Even with plenty of attention, a coriander plant will often not live that long – this is not a plant you will be handing down to your descendants. So if you love to bung some into your burritos or your balti, you might want to stagger planting the seeds so you always have a new, up-and-coming plant ready to take the place of another that's on its way to the great compost heap in the sky.

TIP: Coriander/cilantro plants look great growing in an old colander. The holes in the side provide perfect drainage and you can pop it in a bowl at watering time. Or leave it in there all the time – it's a great way of creating drainage in a container that you can't make holes in.

FENNEL

Skill level	Time	Light	Water
Medium	Medium	Bright	Regularly

Along with dill and coriander/cilantro (see page 124), fennel is a herb that really splits the room. It has a mild aniseed flavour that is often paired with fish. (Though some people think it should be paired with nothing at all!) It's a member of the carrot family and its fine, lacey leaves do look a bit like carrot tops. Fennel has long been used to aid digestion – try a fresh fennel tea next time you feel like you've overdone it with the carbs.

Sweet fennel is grown for its leaves, flowers and seeds. Plant the seeds in a tray, thin out the seedlings and then transfer into their own pot or sow the seeds into a paper pot (see page 22) so you can plant the whole thing into a new container when the plant is big enough. The advantage of this is that you don't need to disturb the roots, which fennel really doesn't like. Bear in mind it will need a fairly deep pot, as the roots grow deeper than many herbs and the plant can reach 30 cms (12 inches) tall.

The other main type of fennel is Florence fennel, sometimes called *finocchio*. This is the one where you eat the bulb, often fried or roasted. It can be tricky to grow a bulb indoors, but the leaves of this type of fennel are just as tasty, and a store-bought fennel bulb provides us with a herby hack. Cut through the middle of the bulb, leaving 3–4 cms (roughly 1–1.5 inches) at the bottom, root end of the bulb. Put it into a shallow dish of water, cut end down, and within a week it should be starting to sprout. You can leave it in water or, when it is well-sprouted, transfer it into a pot of compost and trim off a few leaves at a time.

AVOCADO

Skill level	Time	Light	Water
Medium	Needs patience	Bright	Regularly

The ultimate free houseplant. Admittedly, when grown indoors, an avocado plant is unlikely to produce fruit, but its large, oval, bright green leaves look lovely, it's fairly fast growing and you get the satisfaction of growing a plant from something you would otherwise have thrown away.

When it comes to getting the stone to sprout, the classic method is the best. First peel the brown skin away. Now get some toothpicks or cocktail sticks and with the pointy end of the stone up, press them into the sides of the stone at a slight downward angle. Or use a wine cork cut into two pieces lengthwise as a wedge. The stone will then balance over a glass or jar which should be filled with water so it touches the bottom of the stone. Keep an eye on the water level so the stone doesn't dry out. When it has a decent root, pot it up in a container that's at least 30 cms (12 inches) across.

When the stem reaches 15 cms (6 inches), cut back by half and then, when it gets to around 30 cms (12 inches) tall, pinch out the two newest sets of leaves at the top. Avocado plants can get a bit lanky, so they may need their top leaves pinching out again from time to time. Generally, it would prefer not to be too wet or too dry. In the summer, feed your plant every couple of weeks and give it a bit more water than during the rest of the year.

GINGER

Skill level	Time	Light	Water
Medium	Medium	Medium	Regularly

Hands up who knows what a ginger plant looks like? Despite the fact that ginger is easy to buy around the world and is used as a flavour in many cuisines, most people outside of Asia wouldn't recognize a ginger plant if they saw one.

Well, a ginger plant has tall-ish, slim and elegant stalks, a few of which grow up from each rhizome – what we often think of as the root but which is actually a subterranean stem. The leaves are long and pointed and tend to be dark green, and they have a delicious gingery smell, too.

But is it worth growing ginger when it can be bought so cheaply and easily? Apart from the fact that it makes for a really interesting-looking houseplant, it's fast growing and needs less light than a lot of indoor plants grown for eating. Plus, when you come to harvest it fresh from the pot you'll notice it has a gentler, less fiery and almost floral taste – it's delicious finely sliced in all sorts of dishes and drinks (and you can use the leaves, too).

Take a decent-sized piece of store-bought ginger and lay it down in a wide, shallow pot filled with compost and with good drainage (you want to choose a piece with a few 'eyes' or white points starting to emerge, as this is where the new roots and shoots will come from). Cover it over with a couple of centimetres (an inch) of soil and water well. Ginger is a tropical plant and used to warm, humid places with heavy rainfall. You can start to carefully harvest parts of the new rhizome after the plant is five months old. If it starts to look like it might not survive the winter, then you can take out the whole thing, use the rhizome and start again the following spring.

JASMINE

Skill level	Time	Light	Water
Medium	Needs patience	Bright	Regularly

When jasmine is in bloom, its tiny pinky, white or sometimes yellow flowers give off a rich and slightly exotic perfume, particularly in the evening. Don't let its delicate appearance fool you, though – this climbing evergreen is tougher than you might think and if you can find the right spot for it in your home it will flourish indoors.

You can grow jasmine from a cutting, but it's not that easy indoors and will take a while. If you have visions of perfumed jasmine trailing around your home it's better to buy an established plant. This way you can choose the right variety for what you want. *Jasminum polyanthum* is one of the most common and it's often recommended by aficionados as an easy one to care for that grows well indoors with a lovely fragrance. Winter jasmine – *Jasminum nudiflorum* – is a good option, too, as it needs less light.

Your plant's new home will ideally need to be bright and fairly sunny. If you have a conservatory or a bay window, this is perfect. Jasmine will put up with less light, but it won't flower so enthusiastically. And keep it away from the central heating. If the room is too hot the plant will dry out quickly and hardly flower.

If you find the perfect spot for your jasmine then you will find it grows and grows in the summer months. You can train it up a trellis or let it cascade out of a hanging basket, but you'll need to regularly trim off new growth to stop it becoming a rather unruly mess.

TIP: Any old basket can become a hanging basket if it's strong enough to take the weight of a plant. You'll want to line it with plastic so water doesn't drop onto your floor, and you'll need to think about pebbles in the bottom or another drainage system, but, that done, all you need is some rope or chain to attach to the sides and a ceiling hook to hang it from.

MANGO TREE

Skill level	Time	Light	Water
Medium	Needs patience	Bright	When dry

J ust as with avocados (see page 130), you're not going to end up with a crop in your home, but you will have the satisfaction of growing an attractive houseplant for free from something that you would have thrown away.

First, the dangerous bit! When you have sliced all the flesh away from the mango husk, take a sharp knife and open it up along the side (the 'fluffier' edge will be much easier to split) without damaging the seed inside or, more importantly, yourself. The seed is kidney-shaped with a lighter part on top. Fill a pot with compost and water it lightly. Make a hole with your finger and push the seed into the compost, with the lighter part uppermost, about 2.5 cms (1 inch) below the surface of the soil, and cover it over. It will probably take a couple of weeks to germinate.

As they come from tropical places, unsurprisingly mangos like warm, humid locations. So if your house is very chilly, you may struggle. However, it doesn't like lots of water. Wait until the soil starts showing signs of drying out before you pour in some lukewarm water. You will also need to rotate your seedling in its pot occasionally as it will most likely try to grow towards the light.

TOMATOES

Skill level	Time	Light	Water
Medium	Medium	Full	Frequently

It's quite possible that there is nothing more delicious than a homegrown, sun-ripened tomato fresh off the vine that has never seen the inside of a fridge. Grow some basil (see page 121) alongside your crop and you'll be able to make your very own windowsill tomato salad, or even add some garlic greens (see page 50) for the perfect pasta sauce.

To grow tomatoes indoors there are a few things you'll need to take into consideration. First, light. Without enough sunlight, your tomato plants won't grow very big and the fruit won't ripen. So where is the sunniest spot in your home? That would be ideal.

Second, what type of tomato plant are you going to grow? If you're lucky enough to have lots of space – maybe in a conservatory – you can grow a vine tomato in a pot on the ground. If not, a 'bush'-style tomato plant will be best. They are stouter, smaller plants that will grow to a certain height and then stop – usually a bit over a metre (3.3 feet). The technical term is 'determinate' (vine tomatoes are known as 'indeterminate') and the thing to know here is that determinate tomatoes will grow all their fruit in one go and, when it's all ripe, they are then done.

You can start sowing seeds from late winter up until just before midsummer. They will take around six to eight weeks to germinate in a tray, then, when they are big enough to handle, you can transfer them into individual pots. If you're going for a determinate type of plant, it's a good idea to stagger sowing the seeds so you don't have one big harvest and then nothing.

Feed them once a week with a special tomato fertilizer, following the instructions carefully. Make sure they don't dry out and wilt – water-wise, they like little and often; and not too cold, please. Finally, although they are self-pollinating, it's a good idea to leave the window open when your tomato plants are flowering to waft the pollen around.

PINEAPPLE

Skill level	Time	Light	Water
Medium–difficult	Needs patience	Full	Regularly

Now, let's get one thing straight – you are highly unlikely to be able to grow an actual, full-size, edible pineapple inside your house. Pineapple plants grow pretty big – you'd need a container that was about a metre (3.3 feet) across for this. But, with patience, you can grow a cool, spiky little plant from nothing more than the discarded top of a store-bought pineapple that will produce an adorable mini-pineapple on the end of a stalk. Grow them alongside other spiky plants such as aloe vera (see page 114) for impact; alternatively, a plant growing a jazzy mini pineapple will make a much more original table centrepiece than flowers.

First, cut the top off your pineapple and, with a sharp knife, carefully trim it so you are just left with the central core where the leaves are attached to the fruit. Strip away the outer leaves. Take the base of the core off and push into a pot of compost, pushing more compost in around it so it sits firmly upright. Water well and keep in a warm, sunny spot, repotting as it starts to outgrow its pot.

Once the plant has established itself, it will take at least a year before it produces a flower that will eventually turn into that much-coveted baby pineapple. This is a plant from the tropics that is just not in a hurry. In the meantime, keep your pineapple happy by feeding it with houseplant fertilizer every two weeks in the spring and summer, and making sure it doesn't get below 10°C (50°F) in the winter.

Once your plant has fruited, its job is done and it will start to die off. However, you may find small shoots or suckers growing out of the bottom of the plant. These 'offsets' are new baby plants and can be cut away and put in their own pots.

DWARF MANDARIN TREE

Skill level	Time	Light	Water
Difficult	Needs patience	Full	Regularly

Similar to lemon trees (see page 151), these guys have some quite specific criteria for their living conditions if they are to flourish. The effort is worth it, though, as they make beautiful house plants. Trees from nurseries will come ready-trained as a compact little shrub-like plant and sometimes already with fruit growing on their branches.

It's worth trying out your tree in a few different spots around the house to try to figure out where it gets the most light. Consider rotating the tree once in a while, too, so it gets the chance to feel the sunlight on all of its leaves. A dwarf mandarin would prefer a fairly large, roomy pot, and well-drained soil is very, very important, as roots that sit in wet soil will start to rot. Experts recommend adding sand to the potting mix. You'll also need to fertilize the soil in spring and summer to give the tree what it needs to form the fruit.

Mandarin trees will flower in the winter and the fruit will follow, ripening a couple of months later. Don't worry if you only get tiny mandarins – they will still look cute on the plant and you can use the grated zest in baking, to flavour fish dishes or salad dressings, or dry the mandarins out in a just-warm oven and use in festive displays.

LEMON TREE

Skill level	Time	Light	Water
Difficult	Needs patience	Full	Regularly

A lemon tree is like a fussy, demanding pet. It has a very specific set of requirements and will certainly need your attention but, with its glossy, elegant leaves and beautiful, distinctive scent, a happy lemon tree will amply reward all of your hard work.

The first thing to bear in mind is that all citrus trees need a *lot* of sunlight. So a super sunny spot is vital. Central heating is not going to go down well, so think about how the tree will get on in the winter as well as in the summer. Citrus trees need more watering in the summer than the winter and will require regular fertilizing. And an occasional light but careful pruning, too. If this all sounds like a lot of hard work, then that's because it is. But imagine a lemon tree delicately flowering in your home …

Most people prefer to grow 'dwarf' varieties indoors – this means a regular tree has been grafted onto a smaller rootstock, so it doesn't grow so big but produces more fruit for its size. (Take a look at the Meyer lemon as an example.) But even if you struggle to get your tree to produce fruit, don't despair. A traditional Sicilian dish is cooked meatballs wrapped in fragrant lemon leaves, a technique that works brilliantly for fish, too. The gorgeously fragranced essential oils contained in the leaves also make them perfect for adding to flower arrangements, seasonal wreaths or even homemade candles.

OUTDOOR WINDOWSILL GARDENING

Even if you only have the tiniest postage stamp of outdoor space, with a bit of imagination you may be able to use it as another home for your ever-growing garden. So long as the spot gets a bit of sun, doorsteps, side passages, Juliet balconies and even fences can be used by the clever gardener to produce even more delicious ingredients!

ECHINACEA

Skill level	Time	Light	Water
Difficult	Needs patience	Bright–full	Regularly

Also called coneflowers, echinacea comes in lots of different colours and it flowers from summer into autumn. It's a member of the daisy family and its bold and jaunty blooms have thin petals that droop away from the central cone. Some varieties have a honey-like scent. Echinacea is a tough old plant once it gets established and it works well in outdoor containers and window boxes so long as they are fairly deep. It's a good idea to put some small stones in the bottom to help with drainage.

Echinacea has been used for hundreds of years to fight infections and boost the immune system. These days, many people take it to ward off colds. The plant comes from North America, where it was used as a traditional remedy by Native Americans to deal with snake bites, ulcers and sores. Although there's limited data available from scientific studies to back this up, there is some suggestion that there might be something in it where the purple variety *Echinacea purpurea* is concerned, but we don't know how or why.

If you want to give this traditional remedy a go, both the leaves and the root can be used to make tea. It's a good idea to dry the plant out first by hanging it upside down in a warm, well-ventilated place, before shredding it and putting into a jar to store. Put about two teaspoons of this dry mixture in a cup and allow to steep in boiling water for around fifteen minutes before straining. Drink, and think healthy thoughts.

VERTICAL GARDENS

Skill level	Time	Light	Water
Difficult	Medium	Bright	Often

At its simplest, the term 'vertical gardening' means simply growing 'upwards' – stacking plants and pots almost on top of each other so you can grow much more in a small space. If you live in a city, you'll probably have noticed that some buildings now have 'living walls', with often a whole side covered in plants, as a natural way of dispelling the heat that radiates from concrete and improving the air quality.

Vertical gardening inside your home could be as simple as hanging some pots from a coat hook or towel rail on a sunny wall in your kitchen or dedicating a few shelves of a ladder bookshelf to your plants. However, if you have even a little bit of outdoor space that gets some sun, why not use the vertical garden technique to really make the most of it?

If you can get hold of a wooden shipping pallet, a hammer and some nails, it's easy to create a vertical herb garden (just make sure the wood hasn't been treated with any unpleasant chemicals, as they could end up in the soil). There are plenty of tutorials online.

Screw hooks to a fence and hang repurposed tin cans with holes punched in the bottom. So long as they don't get too hot or you don't let them dry out too much in the summer months, this is suitable for all sorts of plants.

An old frame ladder makes a perfect set of 'shelves' for your plants, and with a bit of thought you can cram a surprising amount of plants onto its steps. How about also suspending a hanging basket from the middle? This works indoors too, of course, if you have the space – but don't forget to think about what will happen to the run-off at watering time!

HANGING-BASKET STRAWBERRIES

Skill level	Time	Light	Water
Difficult	Medium	Bright	Often

Growing strawberries above the ground is not just a space-saving hack for fruit-lovers with tiny gardens, it's actually a really good way to keep them out of harm's way and get a good crop. Unsurprisingly, we're not the only ones who find strawberries delicious – they can be a magnet for pests, so even gardeners with lots of space often take this approach.

The first thing to do is to make sure your hanging basket has a plastic liner – or add one if it doesn't. Strawberries need lots of water and don't like to dry out; you may even need to water them twice a day when it's super hot. But try to avoid the leaves – it's much better to water directly into the roots. If you have a large basket, you may be able to fit three plants in, or just go for one or two if it's smaller. The main thing is to make sure you plant them up so the soil in the basket is at the same level as it was when they were in their pot – in other words, don't bury them or leave their roots exposed.

As your precious strawberries start to ripen, don't forget that not *all* of the competition is going to be foiled because you are growing them off the ground. You can bet that, in nearby trees, birds are watching them gradually turn red with just as much interest as you are! So you may want to consider placing some netting around your plants, before someone else reaps the rewards of all your hard work ...

DOORSTEP POTATOES

Skill level	Time	Light	Water
Difficult	Needs patience	Bright	Regularly

First of all, you are going to need a container that's at least 40 cms (16 inches) deep – some people like to use old buckets, bins or sacks, or you can buy special bags for the purpose. The main thing to bear in mind is drainage: you'll have to water your potatoes quite a lot in warm weather and the water will need somewhere to go.

In early to mid-spring, buy your 'seed' potatoes from a nursery. Small varieties bred for smaller spaces work best. Each potato plant needs about 10 litres (2.2 gallons) of soil, so you won't need many. Before you plant them, you'll need to sprout them. Lay them on their sides in an egg box with the majority of the 'eyes' – the indentations where the sprouts will come from – facing upwards. After about a week they should have some decent sprouts, showing you they are ready to plant.

Fill the container about a third of the way with compost (you will want to do this in the spot where it's going to live – it will get seriously heavy!). Poke the potato about 5 cms (2 inches) into the soil, 15 cms (6 inches) from the next potato and not too close to the edge – these guys need personal space!

Every time the plants get to be about 12 cms (4.5 inches) high, add more compost to the container, without covering the new shoots entirely. Repeat every time they get to this height until you get to the top. Then make little hills around the stem of the plant – you really want to avoid any light at all getting down to your potato crop.

When the plants start to die off – between two and four months after planting – your potatoes are ready to harvest. Pull on the stem and a string of small, grubby jewels of potatoes will appear, like a magic trick!

TOM THUMB PEAS

Skill level	Time	Light	Water
Difficult	Medium	Bright	Regularly

These traditional little pea bushes are adorable and are a great use of a slither of patio space, or even an outside window box. Thanks to the fact that they only grow to about 20 cms (8 inches) tall and yet produce a generous crop, gardeners have been growing Tom Thumb peas in modest spaces for more than 150 years.

You can sow the seeds indoors in trays or newspaper pots (see page 22) in the last days of winter, or to celebrate the coming of spring! Follow the packet instructions and then, when they are ready, plant them out in your container. Don't forget that any shoots that aren't up to planting out will be delicious in a salad. You can also plant the seeds directly into your container if you wait until the threat of frost has passed.

Tom Thumb peas are what's called an heirloom variety – this means that they are not hybrid plants and you can grow new plants from the peas produced by your last crop. At the end of the growing season, put out the whole plant with the last pods still attached and hang it somewhere to dry. When the pea pods seem dry, pod the peas and leave them somewhere to finish drying out completely and then store away ready for next year. Peas forever!

VISUAL INDEX

Aloe vera 114

Avocado 130

Baby spinach 35

Basil 121

Bean sprouts 38

Beetroot 31

Boston fern 80

Broccoli 30

Buckwheat lettuce 41

Carrot tops 44

Celery 47

Chamomile 111

Chard 30

Chervil 82

Chillies 97

Chives 65

Coriander/cilantro 124

Doorstep potatoes 165

Dwarf mandarin tree
148

Echinacea 156

English ivy 76

172

Fennel 127

Garlic greens 50

Ginger 133

Hanging-basket
strawberries 162

Jasmine 136

Kale 31

Lavender 108

Lemon tree 151

Lemongrass 85

Lettuce 53

Makrut (kaffir)
lime tree 100

Mango tree 139

173

Microgreens 26

Mint 68

Oregano 88

Parsley 91

Pea shoots 32

Pineapple 145

Purple basil 30

Radishes 56

Rainbow chard 59

Rocket/arugula 62

Rosemary 71

Sage 94

Snake plant 78

Succulents 103

Thyme 118

Tomatoes 142

Tom Thumb peas 168

About the illustrator

Annie Davidson is a Melbourne-based illustrator
whose drawings have appeared on textiles, picture
books, shop windows and stationery around the world,
with clients including Lonely Planet and Converse,
among others. She is inspired by Japanese woodblock
prints, botanical art and nature – especially forests,
tropical landscapes, coral reefs and cactus gardens.
You can see more of her whimsical illustrations on
her Instagram, @anniesarahdesign, or on her website,
www.anniedavidson.bigcartel.com.